Rainer Krumm

30 Minutes

Value-oriented leadership

Bibliographic information from the German National Library
The German National Library lists this publication in the German National Bibliography. Detailed bibliographic information can be found online at http://dnb.d-nb.de.

ISBN 978-3-96739-086-8

Cover design: die imprimatur, Hainburg
Cover concept: Martin Zech Design, Bremen
Editing: Happenstance Type-O-Rama, Oakland, USA
Set: Zerosoft, Timisoara (Romania)
Printing and processing: Print-on-demand

First published under the title "30 Minuten Werteorientiertes Führen" in 2014by GABAL Verlag Germany

www.9levels.com

You'll know more in 30 minutes!

This book is designed to enable you to absorb concise and sound information in a short time. With the help of a guidance system, you will be led through the book. This will allow you to grasp the essentials within your personal time allotment (from 10 to 30 minutes).

Short reading time

You can read the whole book in 30 minutes. If you have less time, read only those passages that contain important information.

- **All important information is printed in grey.**

- Key questions with page references at the beginning of each chapter allow for quick orientation: you turn directly to the page that closes your knowledge gap.

- *Numerous summaries within the chapters allow for skimming.*

- The "Fast Reader" at the end of the book summarizes all important information.

- An index makes it easier to find what you are looking for.

Contents

Preface

Everyone—whether in the role of customer, employee, or supplier, or in a private context—prefers to surround him- or herself with people who share the same values. In this association of like-minded people, people feel comfortable, are happy to contribute their knowledge and ideas, and are open to the opinions of others. What does this mean for value-oriented leadership?

Any company that wants to be successful today must use its corporate values to meet not only the expectations of its shareholders but also those of its employees and the public. If employees can identify with the corporate values of their employer, they are more willing to work for the company. Conversely, employees cannot fully stand behind a company and the work they do for it if it is not aligned with their values.

However, the figures are what is decisive for companies today—unfortunately, people are usually not taken into account. If employees perform well, they are worth the money. If they do not perform well, they will be replaced quickly. However, many managers have not yet understood that a company, and with it the management, has the power to get and keep "valuable" employees.

If you would like to retain your employees, you must respond to their needs with your corporate values, provide them with a working environment that is conducive to their well-being, and offer a job that fulfils them personally. The same applies to the recruitment of new employees. Values play the main role here because success comes to those who live their values. More than ever before, companies aim to have their values lived by managers and employees and to use these values as a guideline for orientation both internally and externally. Companies must be active participants in carrying out this goal.

But what makes values so special? What influence do values have on our thoughts and actions? How can value-based management make companies more successful in the long term?

I would like to give you an understanding of this rather elusive topic in 30 minutes—because there is so much behind it and it can move so many things.

I wish you much success in value-oriented leadership.

Rainer Krumm

30 MINUTES

1. Value-oriented leadership

Where does the energy come from that all people—but managers in particular—need every day? That strength that is needed when fun and motivation have been used up, all methods have become ineffective, and all tricks have failed—but the task has not yet been completed; the goal has not yet been reached?
The answer lies in values. **Values are orientation variables**, drivers; they are our yardstick for what is right and what is wrong; they are the **guidelines** for our thinking and acting. If values are trampled underfoot, we are not motivated and committed.

1.1 The importance of leadership

Just as we all are different, so too would we like to lead or be led differently. If, for example, our personalities do not fit the task or the environment in which we work, we cannot make the best use of them. For leadership, this means **if leadership is not appropriate to (congruent with) the values, it does not work and triggers resistance from the employee.**
Leadership forms the company within. The management's behavior determines the corporate culture. If the management changes its behavior—as, for example, in a change process—this means a major intervention in the further course of the process, which it can decisively influence. The task now is to reduce the widespread uncertainty among employees through transparency, to provide support and thus guide people safely through the change process. A manager can also act as a guide in such a process, showing how the team can adopt a behavior pattern appropriate to the new situation.

Why leadership often does not work

Although many managers do have the empathy to adapt to the personalities of their employees, they often remain within their own **understanding of the world and values.** However, they have to learn to step out of this in order to be able to immerse themselves in

the world of the company and its employees. This means an expansion of the world of thought.
Especially when a manager changes employer, it often happens that his or her previously well-functioning behavior patterns are suddenly completely out of place in the new position.

Important considerations for leadership work

If you want to lead in a value-oriented way, you have to consider the following four questions:

- At what value level are the company's management guidelines or leadership directives?
- At what value level is the manager?
- On which value level does the employee to be led think and act?
- What kind of work has to be done and what characteristics does this activity require/have?

In order to lead in the best possible way, it is absolutely essential to take into account the **uniqueness of each employee**: as part of the system, with his or her actions, feelings, motivations, values, and thoughts—and of course with his or her abilities. So the **framework conditions** must be right, which will motivate employees to use their skills in a targeted manner and develop new ideas. If the framework conditions are right, people like to work for and can identify better with the company.

The only person who behaves reasonably is my tailor. He takes new measurements every time he meets me, while everyone else always applies the old standards, thinking they still fit today.

George Bernard Shaw

In the following sections, I will first clarify the term *values* and then introduce the different areas of management in order to make the term even more tangible in the sense of the 9 Levels of Value Systems. Then I will present the **congruent management** according to this model by means of the individual Graves levels.

If you want to lead successfully, not only do you have to be aware of your behavior and thus your effect on others, but you also need to know what environment you are in and which values are important there. This fact is unfortunately often neglected. The 9 Levels of Value Systems awakens understanding and paves the way for value-oriented leadership.

1.2 Values and value systems—a definition

Everyone gets along best with the people who most closely share their own values. Why is that so?

We all have certain values that determine our thoughts and actions without us being aware of them. Values tell us whether something is good or bad, whether we accept or reject something that drives us or makes us unhappy. Values give us orientation and support. As important as values are in our lives, they are also difficult to grasp.

What are values?

If we take a closer look at the meaning of the term *values*, the question arises as to what is worth something and therefore important to us. The Latin word *valere* means to be healthy, to be strong—but also to be worth something, to be valid, to have influence. Value therefore contains something powerful for the human being, something that helps people to be and remain healthy. So values determine how we shape our lives and what we consider important.

When we think of values, we consider terms such as *respect, security, harmony, impulsiveness, clarity* or *transparency, status, empathy,* and *tolerance* and many others. Every person has not only individual values but also different rankings for these values. For some people, harmony means reconciling job and private life. For others, harmony exists if they can live in accordance with nature.

If you look at interpersonal relationships, **different values offer plenty of reasons for difficulties and conflicts.** But individuals also can have inner conflicts within themselves because of their values; namely, when they do something or are forced to do something that does not correspond to their values and convictions. If this inner distress becomes a constant companion, this has a negative effect on the person's overall condition. The person is under constant stress, loses more and more motivation, and has already internally quit.

With regard to managing employees, the following extract from the Values Commission's report on the 2013 management survey sums up the topic: "Above all, the involvement of employees in the long-term value process and the consideration of personal values when hiring employees are recommended. Likewise, integrating values into employees' target agreements is an important step towards promoting values in companies. Further measures are: Integration of the debate on values into the training of junior staff, feedback interviews/surveys for employees, and team measures. In addition, the open discussion between employees and their superiors and the designation of clear responsibilities are particularly important. The implementation of values can thus be regarded as a 'management instrument' of the future" (Führungskräftebefragung 2013 der Wertekommision – Initiative Werte – Bewusste Führung, Die Zukunft der Arbeit, Die Wertedebatte, Kai Hattendorf, p. 25).

30 *Values determine our thoughts and actions, usually without us being aware of them. They drive us, give us direction, and help us to decide what is right or wrong. If we act contrary to our values,*

this triggers an inner conflict. In a business context, the consequences are stress, lack of motivation, and inner resignation.

1.3 How are values shaped?

When we consciously perceive a condition or a fact, we think about and evaluate it. This means that we make ourselves aware of what we are dealing with and classify it for ourselves.
Our consciousness begins to mature slowly immediately after birth, and around the second year of life is when we perceive ourselves as a person. As soon as an infant recognizes itself as an independent personality, it imitates the actions and behavior of its caregivers. In the further course of life, other people and groups join in, which in turn help shape thoughts and actions.
As we develop, our values also change again and again—in other words, they shift and adapt to the prevailing conditions.

The main stages of human development

The sociologist Morris Massey (Tad, 1991) divides the stages of human development into three main periodic areas:

- the minting period—from birth to age 7
- the modelling period—from ages 8 to 13
- the socialization period—from ages 14 to 21

During this time, other people have a constant influence on our development and help shape our values. But even after the age of 21, we continue to be confronted with external influences and changes, which also affect our values and their hierarchy (training, studies, starting a career, partnership, birth of the first child, etc.). **We constantly adapt our values to the new environment.** We also live different values in the different roles we play in life: a caring, responsible father can certainly get a kick out of BASE jumping.

30 *Our consciousness perceives a state or situation and evaluates it. In different roles we have a different value consciousness because we adapt to our environment.*

1.4 Species-appropriate husbandry

The significance of *species-appropriate husbandry* is well known in the animal kingdom. It describes the type of husbandry that is based on the natural living conditions of animals so that they can develop according to their species-specific needs, which they have from birth. What does this have to do with us humans? As already mentioned in section 1.2, we seek, as far as possible, to be close to those people who most closely correspond to our own values and who live according to those values. In their presence we feel comfortable, we enjoy working with them, and we are motivated accordingly.

The concept of species-appropriate husbandry from the animal kingdom can—at least at its core—be transferred to value-based management: without species-appropriate husbandry, animals become sick, aggressive toward others, and—depending on the violation—may even die. If employees are managed without a value-oriented approach, they too cannot remain healthy in the long term because the conditions are not right. Their values and thus inner motivators are trampled underfoot. They quit inwardly, no longer perform as expected, and will (must) leave the company. Today, management can make use of this knowledge.

The manager and his or her view of humanity

As a manager, you are inclined to project your own value systems onto your employees. Everyone has their own image of humankind, which shapes their mindset, their self-image. The way leaders view humanity depends very much on what they have experienced at a young age through their **upbringing by their parents**. It is not uncommon for managers to look back on a childhood that has solidified in them the image of being worthless. Even if these managers praise their employees and appreciate their work, they cannot let go of what they have experienced themselves, and they are fundamentally suspicious of other people. Leading people when you are distrustful is practically impossible, but no one would admit this inner attitude. And yet it can be rooted in us.

For this reason, all managers should think about their self-image and their view of humanity to understand why they think in one way or another. If you deal with this and get to know your innermost self, you can be open to value-oriented leadership.

30 ***Value-oriented leadership starts with people:***

- ***Every company that wants to lead successfully today must also meet the expectations of its employees and the public with its corporate values.***
- ***Unfortunately, companies often evaluate their employees only on the basis of figures—the human being him- or herself is often not taken into account.***
- ***More than ever before, however, companies today have the goal of responding to the needs of their employees.***
- ***Values play the main role: values drive people!***
- ***Value-oriented leadership aims to ignite a force that gives employees fun and motivation in their everyday lives, so that they live and pass on the company values.***

30 MINUTES

How can you bring individuals, groups, and organizations to a consensus?

Page 22

Why is leadership so complex?

Page 27

What is the main task of leadership?

Page 31

2. Why value orientation?

According to the study "Leadership in the Top Management of German Companies," only every second employee in Germany knows which **corporate values** apply to his or her employer. Managers and employees of large and medium-sized companies were surveyed. In contrast, all managers stated that their employees were informed about the company values. Keywords such as customer satisfaction, sustainability, or fairness are therefore usually found only in official texts—but obviously not every individual is behind them. However, this is essential for the success of a company: a value orientation lived by all employees leads not only to above-average growth but also to more satisfaction. Every person has his or her own individual values and ideas. The challenge for companies is to **create a consensus**—from the worker to the management level.

2.1 Value systems of individuals, groups, and organizations

Up to now we have limited ourselves to individual values of people and explained how important these are for personal development and that they also ensure that a person can work well and enjoy working—and even rise above him- or herself.

A company consists of many different people. Everyone has their own area of responsibility, is part of a team, and is part of the entire organization. Are their individual values acceptable within their team, and—if so—how are they respected? How do their values fit into those of the company? Does every employee hang up his or her values when starting work and pick them up again only when leaving the workplace?

This is precisely where the challenge for leadership lies: **value-oriented leadership means knowing not only one's own values (leadership mission statement) but also those of the company (corporate mission statement), the employees (employee mission statement), and the customers or market.** It is about the value systems of individuals, groups, and organizations. These become understandable and comprehensible with the model of the 9 Levels of Value Systems, which I will discuss in detail later.

Value systems of individuals

Depending on a person's role and task, **different value systems have an impact on his or her own perceptions and behavior**. In addition, the world in which the person lives and the challenges he or she currently faces are important.

Case study

Polly Plan, married mother of two small children of preschool age, heads the marketing department of a medium-sized company with a global presence. Her department has 25 employees, 15 of whom are based at the site, and 10 of whom work in international companies. She primarily deals with the sales managers of the different countries. In her personal life, Polly Plan is involved as a parent representative in kindergarten and in a nonprofit organization. Before she became head of the department at her current company, she was employed as a marketing expert in a small advertising agency and looked after local customers individually and quickly. The large corporation where she started her career as a marketing trainee had been in operation for 125 years and was too highly structured—which she did not like at all. The world of the small advertising agency, on the other hand, was too restless and fickle for her. Now she is satisfied with the international dynamics, the goal orientation, and the short communication channels of the medium-sized company. Her "thing" is to move and manage issues. She also lives out these value systems in her private life. In her current working environment, it is now important for Polly Plan to find out which corporate cultures or customers suit her best or that she can best work with. Since everyone has several roles at the same time (mother, father, colleague, department head, friend, etc.), **the value systems should be analyzed in relation to profession and role**. Coaching offers the possibility to uncover tensions and areas of conflict and to find ways to solve them.

Value systems of groups

Where people come together, **different value systems** inevitably come together. In the work context this is often the case for teams that pursue a common goal. If even one person is not behind the goal because of his or her value orientation, conflicts are preprogrammed. A possible solution would be to integrate him or her into another department/team that is better suited to him or her as an individual and closer to his or her values. So it is all about fit. Top teams must also be aware that changes in the market (i.e., changes dictated by external factors) can also make **internal changes** necessary.

Case study

For years, the high-quality products of a medium-sized company in special machine manufacturing ensured that the sales team did not necessarily have to sell. For a long time, the sales team was used to customers—who were also experts in their field—requesting possible features from the sales department. The customer was rather captive and did not have to be advertised to. Over time, however, other manufacturers managed to improve their quality. This created competition and resulted in strong price pressure. In the meantime, the customer's contacts at the company are no longer technical experts but management or buyers. After sales have declined rapidly, the sales department is astonished that the tried and tested suddenly no longer works.

Here we must ask: What happened? **Why do tried and tested methods suddenly no longer work?** What has to be changed to get back on the road to success?

Value systems of organizations

For a study on value systems in companies, Werner Auer-Rizzi et al. interviewed managers. The authors learned from one executive that headhunters had contacted his employees and tried to poach them. Although the employees were only moderately paid by their employer, no one responded to a new offer. This prompted one of the headhunters to contact the manager and ask why they refused. The manager referred to the company values: **his employees could identify so well with the company values that they felt a strong connection with their employer.**

The value systems of companies or organizations have two parts: managers shape them and employees share them accordingly. This phenomenon is difficult to grasp. How it becomes tangible is explained in chapter 3, on the model of the 9 levels.

Case study

The two founders of a now very successful company have expanded their workforce to 25 employees at three locations within three years. What was initially very manageable and easy to control with only two people is now no longer so easy to manage. While the two founders were able to manage many things with their intuition at the beginning, they now lack a clear strategy for management. There is friction between the departments, overstrained managers, and poor communication between them. The company wants to continue to grow in the coming years, hire 20 to 30 new employees, and create an intermediate hierarchy.
The circumstances have changed and will continue to change. The task now is to determine the actual state and the desired target state and to put the company on sound footing for the long term. Because in the long run, the current state would mean the company's demise.

30 *According to studies, keywords such as customer satisfaction, sustainability, or fairness usually find a place only in official texts—but not every individual is behind them. But this is absolutely essential if a company wants to be successful: value*

orientation lived by all employees leads not only to above-average growth but also to more satisfaction.

2.2 Values in the psychological levels

Leadership is usually reduced to the mutual relationship between manager and employee. **Yet leadership is much more complex**: every manager is part of a social structure that generates action and reaction. In this environment the manager has a different role in each area: in the company, this is the role of the superior, the trendsetter, the "rock in the surf." In the family, it is the role of breadwinner, protector, friend, role model, confidant, and so on. In associations or other organizations, it is again other roles and values that he or she assumes and represents. Why do we "play" our roles in this way and not differently? The psychological levels according to **Robert Dilts** should clarify this.

The psychological levels according to Robert Dilts

Our thoughts and actions are shaped by different perspectives and positions, which we take in relation to the different psychological levels and which in turn influence each other.

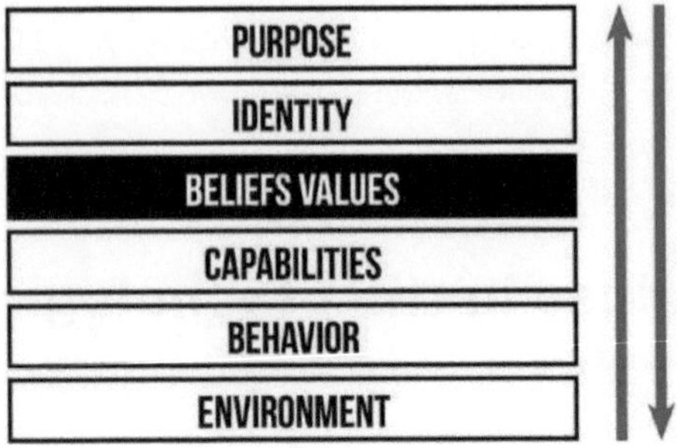

Fig. 1: The psychological levels according to Robert Dilts

Purpose
This level shapes and determines our life and gives our existence a foundation. Here we determine how we position ourselves in family, profession, society, and religion.

Identity
"Who am I?" It's about our self-image, our self-awareness, and what role we play in our lives.

Beliefs and value systems
At this level, we determine our guiding ideas, which we take as the basis for our actions. Beliefs guide our trust in our abilities. And the value systems tell us what is good or bad, what we are allowed to do or not allowed to do.

Capabilities: Skills/strategy/goals
We use everything we can here to achieve our goals with a specific process.

Behavior
This is about our actions, about what we do. This is determined by habits, physical and verbal expression, attention, and so on.

Environment
This is our environment in private and professional contexts, people and objects that occur in it, and so on. Our beliefs play a special role with regard to our value systems, which I would like to explain in more detail below.

How are beliefs and values related?

Beliefs are individual rules (in the form of statements) that we have internalized in the course of our lives. When we believe in something, we feel secure. **Beliefs can either guide us positively or limit us.** Parents often shape them very intensively in their children, who then carry the beliefs with them throughout their lives, because they are deeply rooted in their inner being:
"A girl doesn't do that!"
"Keep a stiff upper lip!"
"Men do not cry!"
"You have two left hands!"

"You don't do anything right!"
And so on.

Values, on the other hand, are positively oriented; that is, they are not restrictive, but motivate and drive us. Values shape beliefs and thus our (positive) self-image—as already described in chapter 1.

Understanding the thinking and behavior of individuals, groups, and organizations is what the 9 Levels of Value Systems makes possible.

30 *Leadership is much more complex than a purely reciprocal relationship between manager and employee. Every manager finds him- or herself in a social structure that generates action and reaction. Depending on the individual beliefs and values that are deeply rooted in each of us and which influence our thoughts and actions, a manager may or may not succeed in leading in a value-oriented manner.*

2.3 The three areas of leadership

Those who are looking for the *best* way to lead, motivate, and manage will give up, frustrated and disappointed. The reason for this lies in the diversity of people. Each individual needs individual incentives that motivate him or her to perform. Each employee therefore also has his or her own preferences with regard to the different management styles. If the principles of their manager match their own, employees react positively to them. **There is a congruence that makes good cooperation possible.** However, if the management style does not fit, there are negative reactions, including rejection, absences due to illness, and internal resignation.

If the general conditions change—for example, by being assigned a different area of responsibility or moving to another team—the employee will also change his or her value orientation over time. And this in turn requires a new management style so that congruence can be restored.

The **main task of leadership** is therefore not to find *the* leadership style but to recognize the diversity of people in their sphere of influence and to align their leadership style accordingly. Leadership is not limited to individual situations but is a **task that grows with the requirements and must be lived.** Leadership comprises exactly three areas that are closely intertwined and must be coordinated with each other:

1. The person (personal leadership)
2. The group/team (group leadership)
3. The organization (organizational leadership)

Personal leadership

Personal leadership is about self-management and also about leading a single person. In terms of **self-management**, the manager has the function of a role model.

How authentic is the manager? What is his or her value orientation? It must be taken into account that a role model has considerable influence on those who are led. The leadership of individuals is the traditional area of personal leadership. As a rule, these are employees who report directly to a manager. **Value-oriented personal leadership means leading the employee in a way that suits both the company and the employee.** This congruence is particularly important in change processes: with the right value orientation, employees can be motivated to support the process.

Group leadership

When two or more people are led, this is called group leadership. Here, the manager has the opportunity to support and shape the behavior of several people at the same time. In this context, it must also be taken into account that the more people are involved, the more different ways of working are required, which ultimately lead to the solution of a problem.
Group leadership is an excellent means of using the individual characteristics of the differently "predisposed" group members to work effectively. As mentioned at the beginning of this book, people always surround themselves with those who are similar to them. This is also the way it is in a group: **the group always comes together because of their interests and can achieve the best results only in this constellation.**

Professor of psychology Clare W. Graves, already mentioned in section 1.1, researched these findings in studies with his students and published them in 1974. His students formed different groups to solve a problem. The loyal ones among them chose the oldest and most experienced group leader. Students who were focused on success and achievement chose the one with the highest grades. The harmonious and cooperative students discussed almost endlessly and then voted democratically. The flexible minded and benefit seekers among them chose someone who could best lead a concrete task—but looked for a new group leader when someone else was likely to be better at a new task.

A comparable behavior can also be observed in companies. **If the management consciously prefers congruent group leadership to fixed structures, challenges can be met better and more effectively.**

Organizational leadership

An often underestimated area of leadership work is organizational leadership. This includes, for example, organizational and process development, but also the change of structures, strategies, or tools. Unfortunately, this area is often not seen as an area of responsibility in its own right, especially by middle management, but is instead more strongly attributed to top management. This way of thinking is a great pity, because the opportunity to influence the success of the company even at lower management levels is missed.

The 9 Levels of Value Systems helps leaders to analyze the current state of these three areas of management. With the help of the 9 Levels of Value Systems, managers—regardless of their management level—can identify why differences, conflicts, developmental standstills, and so on have arisen and learn what can be done to achieve the desired target state.
Everything around us is in constant evolution. Therefore it is very important to change leadership and adapt it to new circumstances. With the 9 Levels of Value Systems, the basic and action-oriented values are analyzed and recorded. In this way, value systems are made measurable, and the usually difficult-to-access values and value systems become understandable and tangible for everyone. A company is successful when the three areas of leadership—that is, personal leadership, group leadership, and organizational leadership—match each other in their value orientation and, above all, match the challenges of the market. Although many companies use the term *customer orientation*, they are surprisingly seldom aligned with it.

If you want to be successful as a company, value orientation is essential. Corporate values form a defined mission statement that provides both management and employees with support and orientation. According to studies, a value orientation lived by all employees leads not only to above-average growth but also to more satisfaction. Value-oriented leadership means the following for leaders: 30

- *to know not only their own values but also those of the company, employees, customers, and market,*
- *not to want to find the leadership style, but to recognize the differences of the people in their sphere of influence and to align the leadership style to these differences.*

30 MINUTES

How do the 9 levels support leadership?

Page 40

How do the 9 levels help in understanding people better?

Page 45

How can you adapt your management style?

Page 53

3. The model of the 9 levels

Corporate success is linked to value-based management—that much is certain. But how does a manager better understand his or her employees, give them direction, and if necessary, motivate them to change?

The model of the 9 Levels of Value Systems provides answers to all these questions. This model represents the development of value systems. It helps people to see the different ways of thinking and behavior of individuals, groups, and organizations and to recognize the need for change if necessary. And it answers questions like, **How does a person fit into a company? How does a team with its values fit with the current task? Is it possible to master current and upcoming challenges with the current values and behavior?**

The 9 levels make values measurable—and therefore changeable.

3.1 The value levels

The human being is constantly evolving. From birth to old age, he or she passes through different **stages of development**. Sometimes the development proceeds faster, sometimes slower. Some people are very satisfied with their current situation and consciously do not strive for further development. Then there are those who cannot wait to change something in their lives. And between these two extremes are all others.

Every human being is at a certain stage of development. We call these *levels*. In the model of the 9 levels there are currently—as the name reveals—exactly 9 levels. The reason for this is that at the moment, it is not yet possible to determine whether another level will be added. Since we are always developing, a tenth level cannot be ruled out. According to our current knowledge, however, we are exactly within the 9 levels. The following diagram shows the individual levels and makes their interrelation easier to understand.

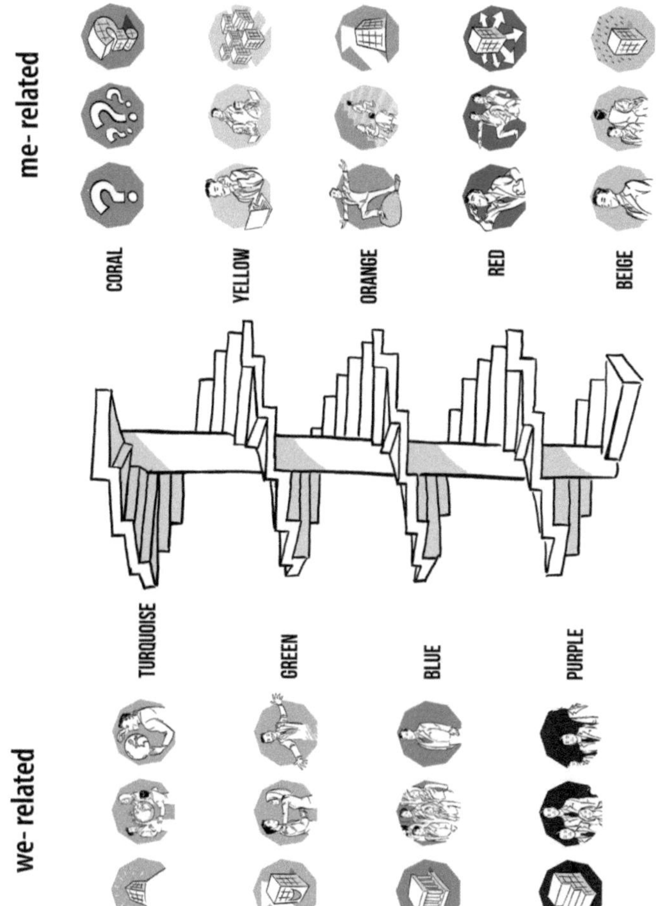

Fig. 2: The 9 levels of the 9 Levels of Value Systems

What the 9-level staircase tells us

The individual levels are arranged in a spiral staircase. On the left side of the staircase are the levels with the WE-reference; on the right side are the levels with the I-reference. In the course of development—that is, on the way up—the human being always moves from the I-reference to the WE-reference.

For people who are on **the WE-reference side, it is primarily important for them that their group or organization is doing well.** They put themselves second and are ready to work for the community. They do not expect a direct benefit for themselves. Perhaps they can draw added value from it at a later date—you never know. So those who are on the WE side are more willing to **adapt to** the environment and external conditions.

People who are on **the I-reference side** are most interested **in themselves.** They are very strongly focused on themselves and think primarily of their own well-being. Their interests take precedence over those of others, and they constantly work to **adapt the environment to their needs.**

At the beginning of life, every human being automatically starts at the foot of the spiral staircase; that is, at the lowest level of his or her development, the level beige. This level is naturally located on the side of the EGO-reference. Newborn babies, for example, automatically begin their development at this level: they have basic needs to maintain their existence (crying out when hungry, thirsty, tired, unwell, etc.). However, because no interesting assessment can be made here yet, this level is excluded from the measurement and plays no role in this book in terms of leadership.

At each level, certain values predominate that determine the thoughts, feelings, and actions of the people who are on that level. Here the human being is among his or her peers and feels comfortable accordingly.

Every step of development leads further up the steps—in rather rare cases, even a step down is possible. On the way up, the values of the previous level are included. It is important to note that it is not possible to skip individual levels. So one developmental step must be totally completed before the next in the sequence can be taken—comparable to the development of a toddler, who must first master the sequence of turning, sitting, and crawling before he or she can safely learn to walk.

The model of the 9 levels is not about one level being good or bad or better or worse than the other. Level purple, the second level, is not better or worse than level yellow, the seventh level. **Here it is not about rating but only about fitting to the life conditions.**

The origin of the model

Clare W. Graves, the creator of the theory underlying the 9-level model, did not use colors in the representation of the levels during his research. Only in the 1990s did Christopher Cowan and Don Beck introduce colors

to illustrate the model using the name *Spiral Dynamics*. The colors have no intended idealistic meaning and were chosen at random. They are a tool for working with the levels. In 1996, Cowan and Beck published the book *Spiral Dynamics* and thus laid the foundation for the dissemination of Graves's theory.
At the end of this 30-minute book, you will understand yourself and the people around you better. Statements such as "typical blue level" will pass your lips more often and will give you an impression of your fellow human beings without judgment.

The levels in detail

After a brief introduction to the structure and functioning of the 9-level staircase, I would like to discuss the individual value levels that are important for value-oriented leadership. As mentioned, the beige level is basically innate and plays no role in the business world. Therefore we start on the WE side in the purple level.

Level 2: Purple

The second-level human is **part of a community** or clan that has a patriarch or matriarch as its leader. In this community the person feels protected. Here he or she gets security and feels a sense of belonging. Everything that happens here follows a fixed set of rules, which exists without having been put down in writing anywhere. No one would question this set of rules.

In this community, obedience and sacrifice for others is required. Customs and tradition have a very high value in this level. In the economic context, one usually finds **patriarchally or matriarchally managed family businesses** with few functional structures at this level.

Examples of values at this level:
obedience
security
tradition
membership
protection
willingness to make sacrifices
belonging
rituals
transmission of lore

Level 3: Red
The person at the red level is on the I side and is striving for **power, independence, and prestige**. He or she wants to conquer and dominate things, and every means is available to him or her. These people use resources to their own advantage and do not care that they could possibly exploit them. Red likes to take the initiative; rules are not respected. For him or her, the strongest wins. Whatever he or she does is only for his or her **own advantage**. The opinion of others is secondary.

From an economic point of view, red is, for example, very successful in pushing forward into new markets and wherever there are hard structural sales forces.

Examples of values at this level:
honor
respect (esteem, fear)
strength
impulsiveness
dominance
assertiveness
winning at all costs
admiration of oneself
aggression
bravery
personal success
independence
self-confidence
contemporary, egocentric thinking

Level 4: Blue
The person at the blue level sees him- or herself as **part of a system of order** that sets clear rules and laws. There is no question for these people about adhering to these fixed guidelines, according to which they live and act. Everything is in order; sense of duty and discipline are self-evident, as well as justice among each other and to the outside world. **Hierarchical structures**, in

which everyone has his or her fixed task, are a must and are not questioned.
In the economic context, large companies are often found at this level and stand behind their quality label—"Made in Germany," for example.

Examples of values at this level:
quality
stability
order
clarity
security
rank/status
sense of duty
law and order
discipline
justice
adherence to hierarchies
control
reliability

Level 5: Orange
The person at the orange level is again focused on his or her own **success**—not only for the moment but also **with a view to the future**. With a lot of energy and determination, he or she works on achieving and maintaining prosperity. In doing so, these people are not as egocentric as the "red ones" but direct their gaze to the whole. Furthermore, they do not overrun third

parties on the way to their goal, and think more about sustainability. Their clear goal orientation ensures that they are constantly and rapidly developing.
Regarding cooperation, they attach great importance to **target agreement** and **process orientation**. Orange is an employee who is committed to making progress in the company.

Examples of values at this level:
career orientation
productivity
entrepreneurial thinking
personal success plus overall success
performance
prestige (status symbols)
profit orientation
added value
acceptance
prosperity
competition

Level 6: Green
The person at the green level also strives to achieve his or her goals, but only together with the team. It is important to these people that they achieve **long-term success as part of a community**. Meetings, relationships, and exchanges with others are extremely important to them. They are open to dialogue and are constantly seeking it.

Decisions are reached by **consensus**. However, before a decision is made, various opinions are sought and discussed. In this level every opinion is important—it takes longer than in the previous levels until a decision is made.
Green is appreciated as a particularly **cooperative partner**. Wherever there is a need for innovation in the group through a lot of interaction and discussion, green people are present.

Examples of values at this level:
responsibility for the other
harmony
consensus
appreciation
fairness/tolerance
adjustment
open-mindedness
commonality/community
securing long-term success
participation

Level 7: Yellow
Up to this point, the satisfaction of needs has been the priority (first rank). From level yellow on, we get to the second rank, which means that from here on, the levels repeat themselves—but on a higher level. From now on, the **focus is on the meaningfulness** of what you think, feel, and do.

While the previous levels include the ones below them—but they consider them to be no longer correct and valuable—yellow as the first level recognizes the value of all previous levels and **recognizes, uses, and combines their strengths**. The levels purple to green have each considered only their own understanding of the world to be correct. In contrast, yellow focuses on multiperspectivity (considering multiple perspectives), knowledge enhancement, competence, and independence. That status, power, or material possessions could result from this is secondary. The yellow type **thinks "outside the box"** and joins forces with those who are useful to him or her—but without exploiting them.

Examples of values at this level:
multiperspectivity
personal development/living growth
autonomy/ownership
knowledge/lifelong learning
creativity
individuality
self-reflection
networking

Level 8: Turquoise

The person in the eighth level focuses on **sustainability and wholeness**. He or she cares about the well-being of the world and does everything possible, both personally and professionally, to support this. In doing so, he or she is selfless. He or she not only observes but also creates.

People on this level manage to hold many different levels together. They recognize things that work together harmoniously and know how to integrate groups and individuals or unite different schools of thought. **They create and protect a whole world.**

To my knowledge, no organizations in the business sector fit this description. Even Greenpeace and Amnesty International are not at this level. Their basic idea usually originated from green. Today, however, they are very blue forms of organizations.

Examples of values at this level:
responsibility for the future of life
systemic action
network intelligence
global reconciliation
spiritual awareness
orientation toward nature
human welfare/sustainability
self-organization of living systems

Level 9: Coral

The ninth-level person is self-centered and believes that all possible boundaries in this world are created by the existence and effort of human beings. Despite this egocentricity, the person at this level does not aim to have as much power and prestige as possible but has great respect for all living beings. He or she also has the gift of motivating other people to develop themselves, to go new ways, and to cross borders. This stage is still in development and is not yet clearly recognizable or interpretable. It does not yet play a role in the current corporate world—therefore it will not be discussed in detail here.

The basic idea when working with the 9 Levels of Value Systems is to recognize the why behind a certain behavior. Why do people behave this way and not differently? Why do you not get along with one person at all, yet you get along great with another person? Why can cooperation fail, and why are conflicts preprogrammed?

30 *With the model of the 9 levels, you can analyze the value systems of individuals, groups, and organizations and thus have a valuable approach for your leadership work. Every person is as he or she is and has the right to be. Value-oriented leadership increases the quality of work by doing justice to people's ways of thinking and not by coming from a self-centered place.*

3.2 Fitting the life conditions

To lead the right or wrong way? There's no such thing. Value-based leadership means leading "in a way that fits the world we live in": the leadership style must suit the employee and the company. The diversity of people must therefore be seen and acknowledged. The 9 Levels of Value Systems helps us to get this **understanding for other value orientations** as well as the understanding to **initiate necessary changes**.

The right management style

Everyone has preferences for certain management styles. If the management styles and principles fit, they are accepted positively. On the other hand, unsuitable management styles meet with negative reactions and rejection. Since the general conditions around us are constantly changing, a person can develop a different psychology over time, provided he or she also has the potential for change. Such a change requires a change in leadership style as a consequence so that the necessary **congruence** can be restored.

When green leadership meets orange employees in a blue organization

If, based on your own values, you like to give your employees a certain amount of freedom to move a project forward, this management style can cause a lot of confusion—provided that the project members are "on track" on another value level.

Case study

As part of a change project in a traditional blue company, Freddy Freund managed a large project. Freddy

Freund's main characteristic in the value system is green. So he led the project and the people involved in it in a very inclusive, cooperative way and without any pretension, because the project should instead develop out of itself. The organization that commissioned the project is traditional, established, and very blue in its structure. The project staff, recruited from a pool of young researchers, were mainly blue-orange in their value systems and expected rules of the game, clear goals, and a good start. What they experienced confused them rather than allowing them to make use of the freedom and scope they had gained. Freddy Freund would have found it easier if he had provided his colleagues with some more goals and rules and then transferred the hierarchical level of the project manager to the cooperative management level. But this way he created confusion, uncertainty, and ambiguity among the staff.

30 *Those who recognize the psychological differences in people's leadership systems and can offer the appropriate leadership style will be able to lead successfully.*

3.3 Coping mechanisms

To paraphrase Albert Einstein, you can never solve problems with the same way of thinking that created them. Precisely because the world around us is constantly changing, we must constantly reorient and adapt. Exactly the same applies to our environment: through our actions of constant reorientation and adaptation, we have an influence on our environment. **So everything is in a constant interrelation.** After an action comes a reaction. Graves calls this "**coping mechanisms.**"

Emergence of change

Each of the 9 levels represents a system in which there are certain preferred value hierarchies and resulting ways of thinking and acting. The hierarchy of values determines how people at this level perceive living conditions and related problems and how they cope with them. If **living conditions or market conditions** change, the hierarchy of values adapts and changes accordingly. New values are also added. In this way, a change from one level to the next occurs.

Reasons for change

Every change often also means having to give up things we have grown fond of, the familiar and proven. It is understandable that this is not convenient for everyone—after all, nobody knows what the future will bring. Fears of very different kinds prevail: the fear of losing power and influence, having to give up possessions, or even losing reputation is omnipresent. So how are changes—coping mechanisms—triggered?

Change does not happen within minutes. Rather, it takes place in a much larger time window and happens slowly. **Change is part of a development process**, and like a process, change progresses up to a point in time when the so-called trigger is pressed and the process is completed.

Such triggers for a person can be, for example, the loss of a long-standing job, a new position, a new employer, the loss of a loved one, and so on. For groups, a new supervisor, a new project, other guidelines and regulations, or changed compensation processes can be such triggers. For organizations, a new competitor in the market, a generational change in management, or the bankruptcy of an important customer can trigger a change.

Basically, it is not important what changes, but that something changes—and that alone triggers fear and skepticism among us: Do we resist? Can we face our fear? Does a superior succeed in reducing the fear and skepticism among his or her employees? Depending on how we face up to this change, it will have an impact on the reaction to the change.

Leadership must also be able to develop and change. If the demands of the world around us change, a manager must also change his or her leadership style in all areas of leadership—in personal leadership, group leadership, and organizational leadership.

A coping mechanism in practice

In the early days of mobile communications, the telecommunications sector was a very clear conquering market. It was a matter of making a lot of deals quickly in order to claim territory so that the market share was secured for the time being. Now, the market is saturated and has become a displacement market. The former management approach—coming from a red world—increasingly had to consider the issue of quality and reliability. Sustainable success was required; that is, a shift from red to blue-orange. Today's customer is networked, informed, and much more critical. The ability to easily take their mobile phone number with them to another provider gives customers more flexibility and thus changes the demands on the services offered by telecommunications companies. And thus to the management: How should the customers be advised and served by the employees? Which salary models will be beneficial in the future? If, for example, employees' bonuses are linked to customer cancellation rates in the long term, the company will automatically lose some red shares.

Because the world around us is constantly chang-
ing, we must constantly reorient and adapt. The 30
same applies to our environment. This so-called
"coping mechanism" determines, for example,
whether and how leadership in change processes
can succeed.

3.4 Why change is important

Change has always accompanied us and made us what we are today. In the course of our growth and development, we understand more and more interrelationships and develop our personality and thus our value systems. The market is also changing; technical progress determines our actions; customer needs are shifting; new job models are in demand. We have to react and adapt to these changes. **Those who cannot or do not want to do this will not be at the forefront in the future.** Change is important—and must meet certain requirements.

Conditions for change

Change always means further development. This can either take place within the current level or mean leaving the current level and entering the next one. Before this can happen, human beings must . . .

1. **Be able to** change (be mature enough for it)
2. **Want to** change (be open to it)

Ability to change

- Is the person prepared to take this step?
- Is he or she able to deal with obstacles that get in his or her way in the future?
- Can he or she consolidate what he or she has learned so far and integrate it into the change process?

Desire to change

- Is the person open to change? Does he or she see the need for it?
- Does he or she feel uncomfortable in the current level and want a change in the situation?
- Does he or she see a benefit in making the change?

The focus of change is always the further development of one's own value systems. Just as important is the question of how this value system fits in with one's own current world. Unlike other models that have to be adapted to new situations again and again, the 9 levels can answer this question. The 9 levels reflect and evaluate stages of development in relation to changes in the living environment.

If these four **areas of action are in balance**—that is, if they are all on the same value level—there is no need for change. However, if only one of these areas changes, an imbalance arises and the other areas are required to adapt accordingly. For example, if the market has changed but the other areas of the individual, group, and organization are still in harmony, a change must still be initiated.

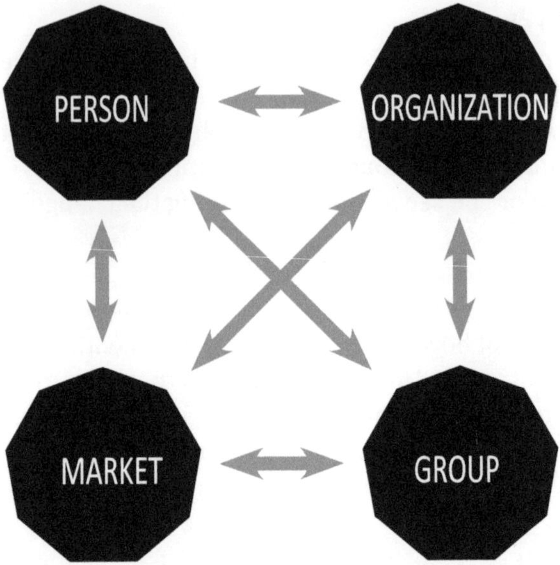

Fig. 3: Balance between the areas of action

Levers for change

It can often be observed that those in charge try to change the behavior of the employees. Unfortunately, this approach is often not sustainable because those affected lack **awareness of the need for change** and the design elements the organization allows do not support this. If changes are to be effective, the value systems of the organization and the people must be addressed. The typical levers for change are the following design elements:

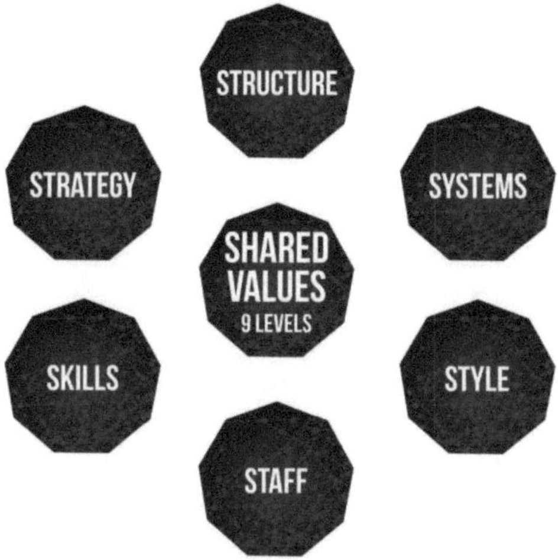

Fig. 4: Design elements for change

If change is to work in the long term, these levers must correspond to the desired value system. For example, it often happens that change is desired, but the path to it remains the same: if the goal is open exchange and cooperation, no competition can be ignited based on old patterns.

If a company is more orange in orientation—that is, very determined and career oriented—people with the same orientation will feel most comfortable there. People who like to have clear guidelines and need rules to orient themselves will perform best in a blue company.

Who wants to be guided exactly how and by whom is explained in chapter 4.

30 *As soon as the general conditions for a company change, such as the competitive situation, customer needs, or technical developments, reaction and adaptation are required. This means that all employees—regardless of their hierarchical level—must be prepared to keep pace with these changes. The model of the 9 Levels of Value Systems helps to achieve this.*

- *Everyone recognizes the need for change.*
- *Everyone recognizes the benefits of this change for themselves and the company.*
- *Each individual is prepared to participate in the change.*
- *Each individual is accompanied through the change.*

30 MINUTES

What is the real challenge for leadership?
Page 65

How do the people on each level want to be led and by whom?
Page 66

How does value-based leadership work in change processes?
Page 74

4. Leadership on the 9 levels

There are certainly many **leadership methods** in the current specialist literature that work wonderfully—as long as they **are applied where they fit**. And here lies the challenge: How do people think, feel, and behave on their value levels, and how do they want to be led and by whom? What is important for them if they want to perform well or if they want to reach their goals together with others in change processes? **In this chapter you will learn to understand your employees better** and get ideas for tailor-made and value-oriented leadership. And please always remember: you yourself are on a certain level of the 9 levels that shapes your thoughts and actions. Your value system logically shapes your leadership behavior. Does this fit the employee and the company context? You alone are responsible for this fit and, if necessary, adaptation.

4.1 Who wants to be led and by whom?

Depending on their individual level, people want to be led differently. If the leadership style is congruent with (appropriate to) their values, ideal conditions are presented to bring a situation or a project to success.
Surely you will find one or the other type of leadership style at your particular level strange or inappropriate. In that case, it does not fit your personal value system. But with other managers and their employees, it may fit very well. Read on to learn who wants to be led how and by whom.
It is important to know that each person is a mixture of different levels. This means that, depending on the role a person is currently in, they live according to the level that is relevant in that context. For example, a manager who is orange in the business context can live according to blue values in the role of family man and, at the regularly held street festival, live out the typical green intention of strengthening the community and cohesion with his neighbors.

Leadership on the purple (second) level

The employees:

- Work long and hard when properly managed.
- Do simple tasks.
- Do not like competition.

- See power and decision-making authority lying clearly with the patriarch or matriarch.

Expectations of leadership:

- Friendly, benevolent, but strict patriarchal or matriarchal management style.
- Clear guidelines, without delegating.
- The boss is where all decisions are made.
- Works with the employees and ensures a good working atmosphere.
- Designs tasks according to his or her ideas and lives them to the fullest.

Not appropriate at this level:

- Too much involvement of the employees.
- Too much delegation of responsibility and scope for decision-making.

Leadership on the red (third) level

The employees:

- Know exactly what has to be done and what the result should look like.
- Are proud of their skills.
- Expect respect and rewards for skills and well-done jobs/fast incentives.
- Want manageable and quickly solvable tasks that can be repeated.
- Want a certain amount of freedom to make decisions.

Expectations of leadership:

- Management style tends to infantilize.
- A clear statement of who is in charge.
- Dominance and strength.
- Shows that none of the employees could do the job better than the manager.
- Employees do not get a comprehensive overview of what is happening in the company.
- New employees are trained—once they are involved in their tasks, no further qualification takes place.
- Creates incentives for good performance (extrinsic motivation).

Not appropriate at this level:

- Too authoritarian and restrictive instructions.
- Too little freedom for the employees.

Leadership on the blue (fourth) level

The employees:

- Accept the superior in principle on the basis of his or her position and hierarchical level.
- Identify themselves more strongly with the company than the employees at previous value levels.
- Do their work well and conscientiously.
- Expect recognition of their performance; for example, through awards.
- Want clearly regulated areas of competence.
- Like certificates and diplomas as awards.

Expectations of leadership:

- Authoritarian and correspondingly directive management style.
- Represents the company.
- Creates a regulatory framework and compliance routine.
- Structures tasks; defines and clarifies rules.
- Job descriptions are clear and unambiguous.
- Employees must be qualified for more advanced tasks.

Not appropriate at this level:

- Lack of leadership, direction, and structure.
- Cooperative management style or discussions (interpreted as a weakness of the manager).

Leadership on the orange (fifth) level

The employees:

- Expect to be rewarded for their work and commitment.
- Must be able to contribute individually.
- Need a high degree of personal responsibility.
- Strive for the company's success, which must also be worthwhile for the employees.
- Want an area of responsibility in which they can move freely (scope of action).
- Are proactive and willing to take responsibility.

Expectations of leadership:

- Competitive management style (reward systems, sanctions, and clear lines of responsibility).
- Transfers extensive and complex tasks.
- Transfers responsibility and grants decision-making leeway.
- Profit-sharing as motivation to be part of a successful company.
- Creates lean and flexible rules that do not hinder the process.

Not appropriate at this level:

- Rewards that are not considered attractive and appealing.
- Not setting rules and limits, not complying with them, and not imposing sanctions in cases of misconduct.

Leadership at the green (sixth) level

The employees:

- Value cooperation with different people, a dialogue with each other.
- Develop and decide together.
- Recognize that they can be even more successful if they pull together.
- Tolerate weaknesses only to a limited extent—will soon be looking for a solution in the interest of all.
- Are looking for a good working atmosphere in which they can be productive.
- Strive for work-life balance.

Expectations of leadership:

- Open, participative, and cooperative management style.
- Being a manager and team member at the same time.
- Must be able to tolerate that even the leader's proposals are discussed and put to the test in a team.
- Actively controls group processes without patronizing.

Not appropriate at this level:

- Putting yourself on completely equal footing with the group as a manager.
- Attempting to assert oneself in the team.
- A management style that is too loose, from which the team could develop an unintended momentum.

Leadership on the yellow (seventh) level

The employees:

- Are happy to accept the guidelines of the management, as long as they meet high quality and quantity requirements.
- Adopt only target-oriented guidelines.
- Love their freedom.
- Want a manager with high professional competence.
- Let their manager know what they need to do to fulfill their tasks.
- Like an open relationship with the manager.

Expectations of leadership:

- Supports the employees in the execution of their tasks.
- Joint discussion of all topics from the task definition to the achievement of objectives.
- Accepts suggestions from employees in order to be able to perform a task.
- Lateral thinkers and free expression of opinion are welcome.
- Supports the full development of the employees in order to be able to commit themselves to the company.

Not appropriate at this level:

- A manager who does not take responsibility for the achievement of objectives and does not provide professional support to employees.

If you want to lead in a value-oriented way, you have to recognize the structures of a team or group and thus understand why the people in it think, feel, and act in a certain way and not otherwise. If you have to adapt to only one employee, the whole thing is still quite easy. However, if you focus on several people as in a department or team, the challenges for the manager are a bit more complex. Here you have to assume that different levels of the 9 levels are represented. In such a situation, the manager has to adapt to each individual and introduce him or her to the common task of the team or group according to his or her needs.

On the one hand, this helps to prevent conflicts. On the other hand, it creates the opportunity to **apply** the different **value systems in such a way that both sides benefit**: the employee, because he or she enjoys his or her work and receives both confirmation and appreciation for good performance, and the company, because it can attract and retain competent people.

With all this, as a manager you must never forget that you yourself live within the value system of a certain level and that this system shapes your own thinking and actions accordingly. Of course, it can also happen that, for example, as a manager with a **new range of activities**—and thus new requirements and employees—you suddenly notice that this new challenge does not fit in with your own understanding of values. The task now is to see to what extent there are discrepancies and to look for **ways to solve** them. And if it turns out that the new position does not fit the manager and his or her understanding of the world and values, it is **better to take a step back**. This is not a sign of weakness but simply the best solution for everyone involved.

30 *Many leadership methods are circulating in the current literature and work wonderfully—as long as they are applied where they fit. The 9 levels shows who wants to be led how on which value level and what the absolute no-go's are.*

4.2 Leading in change processes

As soon as crises and problems arise, management is held responsible for not hearing or correctly interpreting market signals, calls from employees, or challenges from the competition. Leadership is expected to find a way out of the crisis—and this is usually linked to change.

People do not like change—this is a natural attitude, which can be explained by the desire for protection on the one hand and the fear of uncertainty on the other. This is why special leadership is needed especially in change processes. Leadership must be **transparent** enough that those involved understand the need for change and can **actively participate in shaping** it. Yet, leadership in these processes must **exemplify** the **procedure** and encourage employees to think and act in the same way.

What sounds quite obvious at this point is, unfortunately, **often anything but easy to implement**, because even a manager him- or herself is usually too strongly attached to his or her own world and values and trapped in old patterns.

Lack of understanding for the other person's world

Each person moves in his or her own understanding of the world and values—the 9 levels make this visible. This is also the case for most managers. Accordingly, empathy with the employees is correspondingly difficult. For an individual alone, empathy usually works very well. But as soon as several people are involved, the whole thing looks completely different.

If there is a lack of understanding about both their own world and that of their employees, management will never be able to successfully implement a change project. It will permanently encounter headwinds if those affected feel that the developed fields of action are not suitable, and are therefore not prepared to go along with the change or to develop new ideas on their own initiative.

The right approach for value-oriented leadership here is to **know your own value level and to break down and accept the value level of your employees.**

The situation of the company

The **trigger** for the planned change must not be ignored either; that is, the question must be asked how urgent the need for change is. If, for example, a company is on the verge of bankruptcy, the priorities of the management are on a completely different level than if the company is still doing well outwardly and the management wants to make it clear to the employees that a change in the organizational structure is necessary right now. No matter what the trigger for the necessity of change is, **the management itself must really want the change.**

Role model function and orientation

In times of change, leadership has a great **responsibility**. The direction in which the change process will develop depends largely on the leadership. Especially when times are uncertain, when irritation spreads among employees, it is important to offer guidance and orientation to all those involved. Good leadership can do this. Good and appropriate leadership:

- provides support in times of great uncertainty
- guides the employees through the change process
- exemplifies new behavior patterns and actively demonstrates their benefits

The right strategy

In a 1:1 relationship, it is relatively easy to find a congruent and appropriate management style. Normally, however, the leadership meets groups of people of different levels. In order to achieve congruency here as well, a strategy is needed that consists of the following **four phases**:

1. (re)introduction

The management must ensure that the original management style to which the employees were previously accustomed is (re)introduced in order for the employees to understand and recognize everything. In this way, the management builds acceptance and trust. Every employee has the opportunity to see the role of the manager in a positive light.

2. analysis

The management collects information about the levels of the individual employees in their professional environment.

3. congruence

The leadership uses these guidelines to align the leadership style over a certain period of time in a 1:1 setting for congruence with the desired value level.

4. growth

The management builds the elements that are tailored to the individual case into the relationship with the employee, which enables individual growth.

While still in the original management style, employees are assigned tasks that fit their previous work. Now the **analysis process** begins and will continue until sufficient indications of the employees' value orientation have been collected to implement the change toward the desired congruent management style. This is the moment when **development** begins and already at this stage leads to **positive "side effects"** such as higher productivity, better performance, and an improved working atmosphere. At this stage of development it is also possible for individual employees to grow to a higher level. If this is the case, the management will adjust their style accordingly to the new level. Once the employee(s) have accepted the values and behaviors of the new level (in whole or in part), growth is translated into a positive phase. The bottom line is that a positive development can only be expected if all steps of the four phases are implemented. You cannot force a congruent management style. The crucial point is to **find and apply the management style that is congruent with each employee**. Change can work only if it is valued.

30 *Especially in change processes, leadership plays an important role. To ensure that all those affected accept the need for change and that everyone in the boat is rowing in the same direction, leadership must know their value levels in order to be able to initiate the necessary measures.*

4.3 Leading in practice

Just as management tools are used to achieve the company's goals, the 9 levels serve to explain the company and its people. What makes people tick, why one way works wonderfully and the other does not, why people do what they do and nothing else—the 9 levels provide information about this.

The following examples of leadership on the 9 levels will make you see one or the other employee in a clearer light. Or you will see why a particular style of leadership cannot work in this way. Maybe you will also recognize your company/leadership style in one place or another. These practical examples will show you how valuable the knowledge of the 9 levels is—for you and your company.

Showing who's boss

Case study

Robert Reisser is a sales manager in an expansive sales team that wants to conquer a new market. The product is not complex but is new to the market. His employees are dynamic, active, and very self-confident, and they love competition. The whole team is on the level of the red value system. Robert Reisser's management style is also red: he shows dominance and has a role model function. He also trains new employees himself, shows them how to make sales, and is not afraid of difficult conversations. What his employees really appreciate about him is that he can show them "who's the boss!"

When a patriarchal or matriarchal style of leadership fits

In many small family-run companies, the family plays a central role and often several family members are employed in the company. Usually there is a "boss" and possibly the "senior boss" or the "junior boss." If the areas of responsibility in such companies are not yet organized in a way that is based on a division of labor, the purple value system often comes into play here. One works "with the family." The employees are aware that the "company" belongs to the family, that success and failure rest on their shoulders, and that the family therefore has the last word. If the employees feel comfortable under the patriarchal or matriarchal management style and welcome the paternal strictness and paternal care, the employment relationship is congruent. On the other hand, the management has a personal responsibility for the employees and is committed to them—but also demands their commitment as if they owned the company themselves.

Entrepreneurs in business

Employees on the orange level are entrepreneurs within the company. They are proactive, goal oriented, and maximize performance. They think in a networked and entrepreneurial way in order to achieve the goals. This is where managers usually fail if they want to lead with blue leadership values and therefore do not provide sufficient resources and information. This is because these are regulated on the blue value level, and not every employee has easy access to knowledge in this way. Orange employees, with their entrepreneurial spirit, are quickly demotivated if they are slowed down in their enthusiasm and drive. If you want to keep entrepreneurial types in companies, you have to create and allow transparency and freedom and not immediately regulate and sanction in cases of transgression. This is where the expression "delegate responsibility—accept decisions" applies.

Entrepreneurial children found more companies

According to the statistics, entrepreneurial children are more likely to follow in their parents' footsteps and also start their own businesses than the children of nonentrepreneurial parents. Of course, children are shaped by their parents at an early age, and the weekend discussions at the table usually fuel this tendency. So the living conditions shape the value system. Likewise, children of blue employees who work in blue companies also prefer an employer with a blue imprint because they feel at home and secure there. In contrast, orange households also produce orange company founders. But not to ignore the opposite aspect either: according to statistics, the third generation of entrepreneurial children like to drive the family business into the wall. It seems that not only entrepreneurial competence, but also the orange will, is missing.

The team is at the center

At the green level, employees clearly place themselves at the service and responsibility of the team. As a team they push the common goal forward. They proactively assume responsibility. The emotional bond to the team and the team result is high. Involvement and agreements are not just empty phrases, but lived practice. When in doubt, disagreements are discussed again. Managers choose a participative and open management style and rarely make decisions on their own. They often react as *primus inter pares*. In its negative form, it could happen that everything—literally everything—is discussed together and thus speed is lost.

Loose project-related cooperation

Employees with the highest marks at the yellow level are very eager to learn. They appreciate being independent, having competent colleagues around them, and being able to handle exciting tasks. Status and rank are less important to them. Therefore, this level cannot be motivated via the classic motivation tools and career paths. Rather, yellow people want to experience and live out professional competence and complete projects and tasks in that spirit. This does not make them easily manageable in the conventional sense. It is therefore much more a question of providing the right framework conditions that allow performance without hindrance.

30 ***People do not and cannot all want to be led in the same way, because each person has his or her own individual values that shape him or her. A manager also lives in his or her personal understanding of the world and values and is naturally also influenced by these in his or her leadership behavior. The manager alone is now responsible for ensuring that his or her leadership behavior matches the value levels of the employees. The employees at each level have . . .***

- *preferences and dislikes with regard to task management, work attitude, competencies, responsibility, and so on,*
- *a different approach to success and defeat,*
- *different expectations regarding good performance,*
- *different expectations of leadership and the person who leads,*
- *completely different no-go's in terms of leadership style.*

Leadership has to adapt to each individual and introduce them to the common task of the team or group. A challenging task but one that produces enthusiastic employees!

Fast reader

1. Value-oriented leadership

Any company that wants to be successful today must meet the expectations of not only its shareholders with its corporate values but also those of its employees and the public. If employees can identify with the corporate values of their employer, they are also more willing to work for the company.
However, the numbers are decisive for companies today—unfortunately, people are usually ignored. If employees perform well, they are "worth the money." If they don't, they are quickly replaced. However, many managers have not yet understood that a company, and with it the management, has in its own hands the power to get and keep "valuable" employees. If you want to keep your employees in your company, you have to respond to their needs with your corporate values and offer them a job that fulfills them personally.

Value-oriented leadership is the key term here.

Values are orientation parameters and guardrails for our thinking and acting. Leadership often does not work because the manager lives in his or her own understanding of values and usually cannot immerse him- or herself in the values and world of the employees. The 9 Levels of Value Systems helps leaders to understand the values of each individual employee, a group, or an entire organization and paves the way for value-oriented leadership. Value-oriented leadership . . .

- ***is holistically oriented; that is, it is based on the personality of the employees,***
- ***is an orientation parameter for the employees,***
- ***offers guidelines for the employees' thinking and acting,***
- ***tries to influence the target aspiration level of the employees,***
- ***strives to change the needs and preferences of employees.***

2. Why value orientation?

Studies in large and medium-sized companies have shown that although all managers think that employees are informed about the company's values, only half of the salaried employees with and without management responsibility agree with the defined mission statement. So clearly not every individual is behind it. This is fatal for the success of a company.

The challenge for companies is to create a consensus from the bulk of the employees' individual values and ideas. This is because a value orientation lived by all employees leads not only to above-average growth but also to more satisfaction.

30 ***Value-oriented leadership is positively oriented; that is, it does not restrict, but motivates and drives. It is not exclusively limited to individual situations but is a task that grows with the demands and must be lived. Value-oriented leadership does not look for* the *leadership style but ...***

- ***recognizes the diversity of people in their sphere of influence,***
- ***aligns the management style to suit the people.***

3. The model of the 9 levels

As a manager, you can learn to understand your employees better, give them orientation parameters, and if necessary, motivate them to make changes—with the model of the 9 Levels of Value

Systems. This model represents the development of value systems and people.
It provides answers to questions such as, How does a person fit into a company? How does a team with its values fit the current task? Is it possible to master current and upcoming challenges with the current values and behavior? The 9 levels make values measurable—and therefore changeable.

30

If framework conditions, such as the market, technical developments, new job models, or customer needs, change, a company must react and adapt. This also means taking all employees with it—from the worker to the management—so that everyone is moving full steam ahead in the same direction. The 9 levels help leaders to . . .

- ***recognize the need for change,***
- ***see the benefits of this,***
- ***prepare people to participate in change,***
- ***accompany people through the change.***

4. Guidance on the 9 levels

Depending on their individual value levels, people think, feel, and act differently and want to be led accordingly. On each of the 9 value levels, people have certain work patterns, expectations of lea-

dership, and feelings about inappropriate leadership behavior. If this fits, one speaks of value-oriented leadership.

30 ***If you know and understand the structures of your team or group and the people in it, you can lead in a value-oriented way.***

- ***The employees perform their tasks well and gladly.***
- ***The performance of the employees is valued.***
- ***The company can inspire and retain good employees.***
- ***Conflicts are prevented.***
- ***Change processes are managed with the appropriate transparency.***
- ***The leadership lives the process of change.***
- ***The manager becomes aware of his or her own values.***

The author

Rainer Krumm, managing director of the 9 Levels Institute for Value Systems and axiocon GmbH, is a management trainer, consultant, coach, and author. He has advised, trained, and coached international companies, managers, and teams in over 23 different countries.

He is considered one of the most experienced international consultants and trainers in the field of corporate culture and change management—based on the developmental psychology of Prof. Clare W. Graves. With the model of the 9 levels, he has developed an analysis tool that makes value systems of individuals, groups, and organizations tangible and measurable.

He has published several books about the value-based theory of Clare W. Graves.

Contact:
9 LEVELS INSTITUTE FOR VALUE SYSTEMS
GMBH & CO. KG; Ravensburg, Germany
rainer.krumm@9levels.com
www.9levels.com

Related literature

- Auer-Rizzi, W./Blaszejewski, S./Dorow, W./Reber, G./Laufer, H.: Studie „Unternehmenskulturen in globaler Interaktion - Analysen, Erfahrungen, Lösungsansätze", Wiesbaden, Gabler Verlag, 2007

- Bär, M./Krumm, R./Wiehle, H.: Unternehmen verstehen, gestalten, verändern - Das Graves-Value-System in der Praxis, Gabler Verlag/Springer Fachmedien Wiesbaden GmbH, 2010

- Bucksteeg, M./Hattendorf K. Führungskräftebefragung 2012, Wertekommission, Bonn, 2012

- Beck, D. E./Cowan, C. C.: Spiral Dynamics - Mastering Values, Leadership and Change, Williston, Blackwell Publishing, 1996

- Robert Dilts: Die Magie der Sprache, Junfermann Verlag, Paderborn, 2002

- Graves, C. W.: Levels of Human Existence. Ed. Lee, W. R. Santa Barbara, ECLET, 2002

- Graves, C. W.: The Never Ending Quest. Eds. Cowan, C. C. Todorovic N., Santa Barbara, ECLET, 2005

- Grün, A.: Führen mit Werten, München, Olzog-Verlag, 2006
- Krumm, R.: 9 Levels of Value Systems, Haiger, werdewelt verlag & medienhaus, 2012
- Rochus Mummert Unternehmensberatung: Studie „Leadership im Topmanagement deutscher Unternehmen“, Hamburg, 2012
- Tad, J./Woodsmall, W., Time Line, Paderborn, Junfermann Verlag, 1991

Index